The Flow of the Poem's Display of Itself

The Flow of the Poem's Display of Itself

Carrie Hunter

ISBN: 979-8-9915011-2-5

Library of Congress Control Number: 2024949098

Edited by Caleb Beckwith

Cover and interior design by Kate Robinson

The cover image is a modification of *Cloud Shadow With Red Diffusion Light During the Disturbance Period (Midday)* (Jena, April 24th 1884), chromolithographs from watercolour images by Eduard Pechuël-Loesche from *Untersuchungen über Dämmerungserscheinungen: zur Erklärung der nach dem Krakatau-Ausbruch beobachteten atmosphärisch-optischen Störung (Studies on twilight phenomena: to explain the atmospheric-optical disturbance observed after the Krakatoa eruption)* by German physicist Johann Kiessling, 1888. Courtesy of e-rara via *The Public Domain Review*.

Author photo by Ann Pedone

NEW YORK STATE OF OPPORTUNITY. | Council on the Arts

This book is made possible, in part, by the New York State Council on the Arts with the support of Governor Kathy Hochul and the New York State Legislature.

Roof Books
are published by
Segue Foundation
300 Bowery, New York, NY 10012
seguefoundation.com

Roof Books
are distributed by
Independent Publishers Group
IPGBook.com

A Note on Citations:

Italicized lines are from or inspired by Marthe Reed's posthumously published *Ark Hive* and also from her essay "'Somewhere Inbetween': Speaking-Through Contiguity" in *Counter-Desecration: A Glossary for Writing Within the Anthropocene*. Italicized lines that are also in quotes are from Marthe Reed and in quotes in the original.

Lines in quotes are taken from John Ashbery's *Flow Chart* or occasionally some of his prose writings, or other poetry.

"Richly Flows Contingency" is the title of a review of John Ashbery's *Flow Chart* by John Bayley, in *The New York Review of Books*, 1991.

"The Flow of the Poem's Display of Itself" is a quote from Charles Molesworth from "'This Leaving-Out Business': The Poetry of John Ashbery" published in the journal *Salmagundi*, No. 38/39, 1977.

Contents

I. Richly Flows Contingency

13 "Adamantine Resort"

15 "Finally, the Memory Became an Object"

16 "Glamour and Chrysoprase"

17 "The Saga of the Sheepgirl and Her Friend the Pelican Merchant"

19 "Gravity Isn't About to Save Us"

21 "Lesser Animadversions"

23 The "Dieffenbachia" vs the Aspidistra"

25 "Psalm Emanating from Some Debris' Psaltery"

27 "All Cakes and Notions of Pleasure Screened by the Past"

29 "Like Hebe to the Rainbow's Gauzy Showers"

31 "Love That Lasts a Minute like a Filter/on a Faucet"

33 "Never Let It Be Said You Didn't Ask for It"

35 "No Discussion of the Circumstances Will Ever Be Possible"

37 "As I Live in a House, and Am So Bound to Its Principles, in the Corners"

II. All Gabled Roofs Will Fall

41 "The Orchard That Was Right for You"

43 "Nurse of the Arcades"

45 "I'll Wait for You Until the End of Time like Everybody Else"

47 "The Chorus of Condemnatory Shrieks from the Entourage"

49 "Less Hygiene, But More Spirit"

51 "Back to the Dollhouse"

53 "Primness of Outline"

55 "And the Woman with Orange Pink Hair Stood Silently By"

57 "The Pugilists Have Returned to Their Corners"

59 "A Reworking, a Scissors-and-Paste/Job"
61 "Dead End Near Where the Coats Were"
63 "Repeating the Oracle: "Repetition Makes Reputation"
65 "Clad in Dimity"

III. Poetry's Anti-Monument

69 "The Usufruct of the Sparse"
71 "Particles Turn Nasty"
73 "It Seems I can't Think" Either, John
75 "Abrupt Elements in the Sun"
77 "The Edge of a Cross-Section"
78 "The Man that I Entered"
80 "Baffled by a Sandstorm"
82 "A Primary Mood of Spells and Rituals"
84 "Dull Plumage of Another Kind"
86 "...In That Lurch Before One Sees"
88 "Harvest as an Adjective"
90 "The Harvest Home Had No Walls at All"
91 "Reading, Apparently"
93 "Periods of Ritual Slump"
95 "And the Sad Birds Walked Away"
97 "Calm Self-Esteem"/"Neutral Benevolence"
99 "Crags and Castles and Honeycombed Grottoes"
101 "With Stone Lotuses and Iron Epaulets"
103 "It's a River and One Must Keep Up with It"
105 "But That's a Small Cataclysm in a Landscape Now/That's No Matter"

IV. The Flow of the Poem's Display of Itself

109 Even the Diabolical Orgiast Has Ascetic Aspects

110 "Ambiguity Seems to Be the Same Thing as Happiness"

111 "The Old Bomb Was Having Its Say."

113 "Personal-Pronoun Lapses"

115 "The Japes of Skeptics"

117 "Something Sweet, Turning Over, Something Unbuttoned"

118 "A Distant Sister Comes"

119 "Like Sleepwalkers Amid the Gaiety"

120 "... and so History Constantly Dwindles"

121 "The Title Always Wins"

122 "As Long as We're on This Planet the Thrill Never Ceases"

124 "A Misleading Index of One's Intelligence"

126 "The Glabrous Drop That Will Satiate Us"

128 "Rejoice in the Exterior Outcome"

130 "How All That Fluff Got Wedged in with the Diamonds in the Star Chamber"

132 "What's Wrong with a Little Pudding?"

134 "No One Calls the Woman Who Walks Silently Away"

136 "It's My Sonata of Experience, and I Wrote It for You"

138 "It Will Look Better on a Cassette"

139 "Each to His Own Bed"

141 "Not Quite Late-Twentieth-Century Panic"

143 "A Doubt Hangs Like a Jewel"

145 "Deceived in our Reckoning"

146 "Mere Grace Notes in This Battle of Stupid Titans"

149 Acknowledgments

I. Richly Flows Contingency

“Adamantine Resort”

A memory that is a story, but then some magical element.
Looking back at a past, and what you hear.

The fly, the key, unclear proper name reference,
“the gunwale unkisses faster,” ammo scuttled,
inhospitable jettisoning.

Marthe Reed’s *illusion of mastery*, Sarah
Rosenthal’s investigation of anti-virtuosity.

The metaphor where we are all a horse.
One-upping the theorists before they can even get to it.

An alibi, foxglove, doves who have been given permission.
A plangent river.

So that all children could have at last
                    what was ours, what was to be ours,
                                        what will be ours///
                                                                  but, we, us///
                                                                                                          will be no longer,
                                        so it will be theirs.

[laborious happiness]
[idiom] that applies to [X] applied to [Y]
[prematurely grey]   [hair]   [slab of expanse]

Two friends gossiping about each other, misanalysing
each other, but I don’t say anything.
What ecoterritoriality is understanding?

Partially indoctrinated into the structure, but not quite.
Or given a structure, but none of the privileges.

We are not separate from the mess;
as if we didn't make it. As if we made it,
but can evade the effects of it.

We are the mess, we made the mess, we are the mess.

The seeming literalness of a metaphor
enjambed together with a sincere but flippant
question.

Enact what you deserve.
Questions where the answer is clearly yes,
but not something anyone's thought of.

Critique of nature writing:
an experience that is only an echo
which leaves dualism firmly intact.

You asked me how my theorem was,
I asked you how your mother was.

“Finally, the Memory Became an Object”

The light patched up later, after the fact.
The conversational you, interjected.

Bright, snazzy, fabulous slownesses, fantasticality.
Skipping a comma just to throw you.
The center disappears in the middle.
The furniture, what we walk around,
                                   use’s communication
                  came to be seen, comes, to seam.

If you view yourself from within the ecoterritory,
and not separate from,
there is no need to replicate the self.

The Patagonian’s love of connections.
The abusive companion trope.
The light splitting apart our structures, mundanely.
Performing your life with no witnesses.

[extremely taupe] [barking low like a hiccup]
We are not only cataloguers, but heirs. Apothegm.

The poem must eat earlier poems.
“Invade each other’s privacy in a significant way.”
Postscript in invisible ink.
Personification of houses, air.

Naps as a metaphor for naps.
The glacier’s job done.

“Glamour and Chrysoprase”

I’ve heard that the subject matter is on its way.

Not saying *exactly* creates a space to pull meaning out of
vs a specificity which is useless.

Memories mixed up, only recognized as such through changing pronouns.

Cataloging the ancestral despairs.
“All of my déjà-vus were ones that could have occurred to him.”
The implication that there is truth, even.

The kind of age we live in. Only one’s first initial.
1st person plural possessive, when one becomes I.
“Meliora probant, deteriora sequuntur” in italics /*“The exhausted trope, ‘Nature.’”*
An undetermined choice vs an indeterminate state.

The poem ending with “you.”
Beginning with music and gender.
Not gender, or genders, but the gender,
as this one amorphous thing that affects us all.

Lovers silently arriving then departing.
Space on Earth and on a bicycle trail.
The “celebratory of what once was.”
Using only the gender neutral indefinite pronoun.

“That an answer actually exists.”

Hems of the pastoral.

“The Saga of the Sheepgirl and Her Friend the Pelican Merchant”

Casual, conversational asides.
Causal film chant.

Archetype’s actions’ academic causal physicality.
[an absence of typewriters, but not of bells.]
Random third person singular masculine’s story.

The dream dismantled, fallen down, crumbled.
That terrible moment when you like your life.
The location given but the location unclear, mythical.

“The esplanade.”
A scene in the dark.

The quasi-natural human, the unnature of nature.
Sullen waiter in place of birdsong.
Analysis of memory. The title of a stray book.

Casual everyday dissociation.
Sometimes it’s just about language: “in the nadir of a pause.”

Music coming like aphorisms from stone —Hejinian

Making a choice, making the wrong one, and being certain
of it. A comfortable privacy, but entering the wrong door.
Pathos, nimbus, limbo.

Precursor to hell zones of experience,
                    being sultry, being adulterous,
                                        vast and unclotted spaces.

Denise Newman's anti-paradise, Dana Teen Lomax's guilt.

Modal of possibility, "your" possible situation.
An old "chromo" on the wall, innocent as a "lintel."

Hate-filled cubicle jobs
          and how that leads to an explanation
                    of what Osiris would do.

How snow is truth and how you show truth.
Against reinvention and for becoming more and more the self.
Votive angel gatekeeper's actions at the gate.

"Gravity Isn't About to Save Us"

Clues fated to not be found.
How you rinse charm from bones.

The difference between disintegration and return.
Awareness as a scientific measurement.

Looking for symmetry or order and having it withheld.
The mythological, but mixed with the legalistic, liturgical.

The disintegration of the form into the previous is not itself
anything new, but just another iteration made out of the same one.

She says, Some words are better in English.
He disagrees that opposites attract, but it also never
works out with people who are too similar either.

Stationary saraband and all the sudden talking to mother.
If I could only understand what the subject matter even is.
Hitting solid objects with shadows.
An atmosphere breathable but tenuous and contingent.

Enough cognates to make us believe in doves.
Time being the subject matter, and where it resides.
"Fons et origo, nemine dissentiente" in italics.

A swoon being a type of rest.
Finding the "good"—a dreary proposition.

Minotaur, slaked blood, sacrifice, and austerity.
Dead wood and an expanding afternoon.
Paralysis takes over as if it's a type of action.

An additional isolation,
as the solution to the problem
created by sequestration.

An unrecognized substitution of [landscapes [of elsewhere]].

A series of questions with no questioner.
One's voice unheard even when heard,
at least in the way it's heard to the self.
A litany that is just your own life.

A quire is not a choir and not quite a quagmire.

"Lesser Animadversions"

On an island together, and it's a jail.
The persona as an "us."
It's like you're them, but not one of them
and they recognize that,
but also you belong there.

How we're privileged via isolation.

My handwriting all around me, as if you're wearing it.
"...accept the face [people] give to you."
The fiction of the ocean.

A quiet mumbling over attendance lists.

"Redo everything," "chatter," "subsides,"
"forever opaque," "a longing one does not subdue."

A quotidian act and how it's monumental now.
Those days, generalized snap judgements.
Realizing that the story has disappeared.
Mélisande.

An effort to let in mythology's muse, but not finding her.
All that's left is wind.
Progress enfolding you so much
that "you" are no longer evident.
Development without resolution.

"Too fast for compliments."
Advice in a lobby that's not really helpful.

The narrative leaps up in time.
Indefinite pronoun, but we don't know what "it" is.
Its whole isness, I mean itness, is unclear.

Our ecological solutions
        destabilizing,
                harming biodiversity,
                        soil health.

The vexed questions continue.
That their erroneous impression is actually true.
"Harvested, but still sitting around."

The lake's opposite shore's lost object.
In the palm of your hand.
"Easy definitions and only so-so resolutions."
Taking the path of giving up.

Green water.   Blue sky.   Gold leaf.

Pencil shavings vs. dead tea-leaves.
Philosophical rantings about what constitutes
a social event.

Problematic nature writing.

Steal what you can before the stark light comes back.

The "Dieffenbachia" vs the Aspidistra

The difference between planning future actions
and practicing for the perfect Kairos moment.
Daydreaming away the perfect future
that doesn't exist.

Shocked clocks doing their being.
Life in the dead leaves.
That moment when you realize the poem is a letter.
Pampering the abandoned.

A confusing heterosexual narrative embedded in one
that cannot be. The sunset's delay striking terror.
"A basso-profundo fibrillation."

"...no closer to complex interpenetration."

A list of things that made the homecoming truly grand.
The problematic included.
The end result unimportant
compared to the process
of getting there.

The twilight, lost.
Too young and refused admission to the bar,
lying face-up on the street, missing you.
"Uneventful," but don't look
at what my heart's been through.

Having forgotten your theory, but still
researching and trying to prove it anyway.

Eureka with mistakes. Eureka,
a madness. Collapsing into objectivity/
subjectivity. How one is helped along in their work.

They expect you to do what they are not expecting.
Windlasses are not women of the wind.
A summary is not necessarily a translation that is comprehensible.

Is nature an environment or (a) being?

Reading backwards to find the subject.
Earth's felicitous result.
The river sometimes disappears
when the obstacles prove to be too much.

"Like a moraine"—your life never what you thought it was.
Just the desire to sing is enough.
Escaping into a future I want is not exactly satisfying.
Excommunication, society a stronghold.
The word you're forced to pronounce.

The third landscape is of things.

"It doesn't seem anything/can establish itself
as the slab of meaning I feel central to my situation."

Déjà vu in nature/of the landscape.
Not the real me; "to rain past thirst."

"Psalm Emanating from Some Debris' Psaltery"

A visitor is OK, but a lot of other things are not OK.
Sympathy, frightening.
Concern about gardening, keeping a lid on it, manners.

A poem that is a letter, but the reader of the poem is missing
information that the reader of the letter would have.
Palimpsest of consciousness.

Isolating privilege. Those imsolated within privilege.

The disinterest of logic's emotionality.
Desire to be exchanged, I will go.
As if you or whatever "she" there is, is a hostage.
Take me instead.

"We have no way of forcing others to cooperate
except by vaguely acquiescing to their most intimate desires
and pretending we don't know what it's all about."

Suspicions unconfirmed, action diverted,
so all you can do is stand still, give your speech.
The paperweight rolling, snow falling upward
because sagebrush, engulfed in snow.

Damaged interrelations due to the classification of "human."

A semblance of time, luck turning, doesn't mean for good,
just this is what happens next.
More terrible events, fate, nature's waters hissing.
But when everything's rolling, it keeps on rolling
and will eventually roll past, won't it?

Paperweight,
sagebrush,
bunkhouse,
a warrant,
refund hiss,
rolling fire ants,
billows mandibles.

Who survives is no better than who does not;
it's just incidental.
Some sort of static intermediary place
between work and church. Every extracurricular
activity is intracurricular.

The anthropocene restructured.
Fantasy of restructuring from within
because from without is illusionary.
The only option really is to smash structures,
but the anthropocene is not a structure, so how
could it be smashed?

The blinding horizon stands in the way —Hejinian

What you would do differently from others.
A lot of large pieces on the freeway today.
Meditation on remaining single.
Teetering on the edge of forgiveness.
Also, fluff. Or at least wooly.

“All Cakes and Notions of Pleasure Screened by the Past”

All of the sudden, dialect.
Petty but also important accusation.
What saves you is a ghost,
and so is the saving, itself, even real?

Interlocutor there, interloper here.
The retrieved’s missing parts.
The self given back to you in partialities.

Devoted to or at least agreeing to the secret, secretly,
our downfall.
A severity without greeting.
How reassurance incompletes us.
The list revealed as a list of heaven. Pathway into.
Roseate flames point toward.

The topic geographical, polis is this.
Something amiss, but as if nothing was.
A rusted tackle indicative of a lost owner,
not a faded-away rendezvous.

As if the mountains had a motto,
and we obediently buy what they’re selling.

Difference as intimacy.

Not my lot, tilefish, beckoned, loitering.

Long lines that purposefully force spaces that wouldn’t
otherwise exist.

Those who live without assurances, and those who wonder why.
Mutual gratitude's pointlessness or the skewered perception thereof.
Revenge in A minor, muted, underneath.
Middle C's politeness.

//Getting even *with* or getting revenge *on*//
//People you've just met//

Decentered anthropomorphism.

Ebbed not fused. A spontaneous privacy.
A secret daily routine, but not really secret,
just unremarked upon.

And in the utopian future that is only a safe haven for
my terrible present, I told him a secret. Really, any secret.
Everything I know and I am, almost, is a secret.

The last fractioning outcome.
Of course, split decisions can never be planned.

"Radical diffusion."

I know I'm peaceful when I only do one thing at a time.
An ambience of living freely, in the moment.
The lull of spontaneity.
If you went into cafes and I went into bars.
Some post-atrocity calm, sour.

"Like Hebe to the Rainbow's Gauzy Showers"

Trails, incompetency, trellis of clouds
following the sun's slide away,
and city spires.

"Madhouse statuary."
The previous dispelled in dreams.
Variations and textures cannot exist in time or in daughters.

A nice day decreed.
That which is only accessories,
unaware they are central to the entire thing.

The blossoms go away because the judge told them to.
But it's ok for the others, the transitory, the transient,
we just don't say so.

Mary Burger's memory and doubts about memory.

Intermediary between what is allowed and what isn't,
and the place these places reside.
Work, a lot of work, as if you have work
like it is weather or an environmental condition.

An extended metaphor of a common idiom.
A woman's complaint. The hangman suddenly.
Work, doing the work, the problem of the work
and characters coming out of the woodwork.

The "wildflowers in the wallpaper." Taking it more
internal than is meant. Not wildflower wallpaper,
but a hybrid form of two things which would never be hybridized.

Charlotte Perkins Gilman's *The Yellow Wallpaper* palimpsested over
Ashbery's wildflowers.
"Presto, no one was there."

Memory of the ecosystem (genitive) collides
with lacunae of the individual.

Another empty room.
What Joan said too.
Ornery purgative exodus.
The father, and disobediences.
An injunction, chamois costume,
what about when it's really too late.

"Love That Lasts a Minute like a Filter/on a Faucet"

A clear subject matter.
Writing about one's own's writing's incoherence, coherently.

"Do not read what is written. In time/it too shall become incoherent
but for the time being it is good/ just to tamper with it and be off."

Twisted creeper and listing tundra.
Not your subject matter but taking it anyway.
"Things that happen" in relationships.
The gay male narrative's "lesbian truth."

"Together" or "To gather."
"The apricot lamé of the distance."
A cliché as soon as it is written.

The place where we are is a festival. And there are hogs,
and it's possibly Asia, or only Asia in possibility. The owner
of the grain elevator as a character in the poem.
The punishment that you are asking for.

When story as metaphor becomes so much story
that it can't be metaphor anymore. Superstition
Mountains, the Lost Dutchman Mine, undiscovered gold.
The Mineral Springs. Some sort of settling down in nature
forsaking what you never forsook.

It's like some Walden Pond narrative without saying so.
Narrative of a famous text, as if you wrote it, but you didn't,
and also not using their words, but using your own.

Trees have an entirely different meaning in Black history, you know?
so I'm always surprised when I see trees being held up as this complacent

object in nature to avoid writing about political realities. —Nikki Wallschlaeger

Too smart to say anything.
The topic, a heist that took place.
Not sure at this point if it is a metaphor or not.
I don't really believe that Ashbery ever had a barrel
he debated looking directly into or not.

What you must sell out and just buy,
and by the way, you're addicted to it.

"Never Let It Be Said You Didn't Ask for It"

Haunted house with blue shutters.
Only in this one situation
are two people unable to
occupy the same space.
Your future actions unclear,
and ending the page on that.

Christina Sharpe's "weather" of racial violence.

The subject is that there is no truth.
Don't do what they tell you to
if what they tell you to do
always dislocates your knee.

Ashbery's distinguishing between types of truths,
and the truth that does not exist
is the truth that is an occasion,
that has been fitted to an event.

Trash doesn't disappear.

The truth that does exist is the kind that is more
or less appropriate to its time and place—
although it might just exist "here and there."

Sending the scribes back to their tablets.
Framed silhouettes "as I walked in."
Corporal punishment, pussy willows, a sitting room,
a waiting room for crying.

Looking for others to compare spiral notebooks,
apparent politeness missing, children talking,
conclusions not reached.

Anthropocentric white privilege.

Mispronunciation due to mis-parsing the syllables.
Not rag-out, squirrel ragout like a dish.

A kettle. As if one might read by the light
of the kettle but it's too damp to read by.

Marthe Reed's last words to me via email:
Ok, thanks. —April 9, 2018, 12:14 PM, PST

Figures blended into walls.

A casual entrance, probably unplanned, as if just in the area,
wearing a hat even, a casual "having your say,"
so maybe it wasn't a casual happening by after all.
But what this "say" was isn't said.

“No Discussion of the Circumstances Will Ever Be Possible”

But we know it’s not brusque.
After saying what’s needed to be said,
a tour of the house is given.

Fate something that has a home where it lives,
when it’s not going around creating havoc,
and that home is a cauldron.

As if climates are conditions,
but conditions aren’t real,
so climates, temperatures, weather
are not real either.

Mammals, meanwhile, appear when one is relaxed. —Hejinian

What you must do
hovering around you insisting,
but you don’t know
what exactly it is
you must do.

In what space and time
when all is demented
is, certainly, this one.

Those who will not leave you
in peace also not giving you
permission to stay longer.

If she was alive, she would have gone further.

Onondaga territory is not former territory,
Ohlone land is not former. A culture is not past tense.
Thinking requires so many crevices to bleed into,
threads to follow; is never finished.

This coming and going is very much
the same thing to me.

“As I Live in a House, and Am So Bound to Its Principles, in the Corners”

Unfragmentable writing.
But sadly, it’s not to be, so I change my clothes,
accept my attitude, or change it as well.

Bound to the corners,
bound to a house,
and its principles.

When you have to type out Ashbery verbatim,
because there is no other way to say it.

Dream of what might have been
erupted into lightning
in some adjacencies,
but then just accepting worn places/tea
kettles, misted windows, “cum
frumentum” in italics.

Global warming, Marthe Reed, other things
hard to pin down.

The hyperobjective Marthe Reed.

The end that will be commingling in heaven.
In a sort of heaven.
Losing a good idea by not writing it down.
“Yet by losing it one can have it.”

When none of us were opinionated
because we all had the same opinion
of absolute horror against the prevailing age.

Not a list of contradictions.
Not a list of similar things.
No one present
to compliment the sloppy
record keeping.

Tethering the present to the future. —Tyrone Williams

Critique for another time paralleling our own/
or critique in its own vacuum.

The introdution at the end. A book ending with instructions outside of the book. A glossary without attribution, but with a contributor list and their statements at the end. Decentering the author, decentering the anthropomorphic. The painting left unsigned.

II. All Gabled Roofs Will Fail

“The Orchard That Was Right for You”

Setting: The Water.
Shawls, a wharf, a rope, a password.
Smiles are a pattern you wear indicating a dagger.
An outfit, an ensemble. An ensembly. An assembly.
Acquiescent demands. The water a place
to be pampered. The setting not a specific setting.

The coded language of a region inaccessible to the uninitiated.
What we think we know, but we don’t.

Always confusing deictic and enclitic.
Sinkholes open up cleverly disguised.
Everyday mundane questions; another summer
coming to take its hand from the sun.

This is a land memoir.

“Fish tales” is an idiom that means the fish are speaking.
Bluetoothvegetables.
Talking in specifics around a nonspecificity.
Pointed accusations coming to
take their hands from the moon.

Not a space for stopping to think or reconsider,
but something to fall into and be lost forever in.
“That odd, dank furor of attention.”
No sense of time rushing past or other people’s sense of time.

Being the pivot, but stopping just short,
but being adorable. And in the shadows,
the memories of everyone else
who’s ever looked down into

Rivers, basins, lobes, deposits, locks, and levees. The Gulf.

Wishes that are shadows.
Wishes you never remember.
Wish's decline a sort of wholesomeness.
Animistic wish flying but no longer a wish, a bird.
A list of things that are fresh or might be.

A word that reminds you of a previous crisis.
That moment after a sound reverberates.
Negative striation.
We look for a beginning in the wreckage.

Verdancies profligate.

"Nurse of the Arcades"

Question of whether we are at shores or gardens.
There there, she says, or There ⟿ pointing. Deictic.
"It nourishes other asides it knows nothing of."

I don't want to say what comes after. Dancing
after, sidestepping what's passed, is still passing,
passes over us. Tedious crossfading.

Something to escape, or something to escape to.

"My fear is like a small house: you can come visit me/
but it will not go away." Passing through as a sort of
departure. Something is always coming loose in the poem.
Chilly, unripe fruit, timeless or nonspecific time.

Being put to the test, but not now, sometime in the future.
For now, some non-test activity, or battling the weather.
[Not at a] pinnacle of some decision or other.

**Haint* blue, whispers of taint, it is and it ain't,*
what taints, is tainted.

Psychics who are right.
A list of metaphors for building something.
The city and the city's lair.
All lives have battle sections.
Definition of the one and only in horticultural terms.

"They handed us over to it/and we were alone."

The battle scene leads to the Arcadian scene.
The animals, pilgrims, defeated, supplicants, bushes, virtue,

an antidote. The domens, a joke, a centipede, morass.
A beast, a lair. Apathetic wondering.

An unnamable coherence.

Love's crescendo, but inside a fermata.
Fear's wall; a depression.
A man walking his dog with a dog ball launcher,
and I say, "That man is walking alone holding a single flower."
A bird is screeching outside my window. I ask, "What is that?"
He says, "An eagle."

No center, only the circuit.

"I'll Wait for You Until the End of Time like Everybody Else"

No part for you in the play.
Crashing water systems.
Supertankers, cotillions.
Tone-leading structures leading us no one knows where.
Stiff-kneed, a stiff one needed, or a few provisions later,
the momentary stopover.

We are in a predicament: we are in a foreign country (I
don't know where) and we are in theory. —Hejinian

"We make it up as we go along."
Seeing what everyone else sees
for what it was, and that it was a charade.

Knowledge not guarded as much as it is carried.

No tigers, just paper-thin characters "revived,"
a wider denouement. The forces we forgot,
low-lit in the back with the torn wallpaper,
move further back into the shadows, altar to the sun.

"Too late for pie."

Writing verbatim lines in the wrong order.
Nature taunts you, but you only know
what it's doing because it's done it before,
will do it again, so you just wait thorough
for the next one. What is beginning
is what is disappearing. Confabulation
of waiting.

Erosion, ice melt, the reduction of land to an island.

Every day is like Wednesday. Hump day
you never get over, so you write lists, write list
poems, write your unhappiness, sort out the living
that must be got, or must be given, that which keeps
the rest of us disconnected, the board barrier diverting
traffic. You disconnect.

Outsider's guilt.

Your misery is my breath, my misery your breath.
Barely worn, hardly on. Those who can tell what's coming.

List of vegetation. List of endangered animals. List of flavors.

Like Christ's still here, like a leap's still drifting on. As if all
you want is your heart scorched, but no one will give it to you.

“The Chorus of Condemnatory Shrieks from the Entourage”

Pergola, the smile of a latecomer, no insulation, puffery.
The tray we thought was empty.
“Will our pain matter too, and if so, when?”
Maybe it’s only a dirty napkin and an orange stick,
but it could have been more. Lugubriously painted.
Brunch, sloth, suicide.

Segregation’s encroach towards the middle.

So where are we but on the pavement/
flagstones, arranged in clusters. Cluster
headaches. Clusterfest. Clusterfuck.
Where is the amphitheater?
The tipping point//is something you follow.
Cogitation leads to carousing.

Land sediment, flood plain, wetland, fluvial, marsh, bayou.

It only makes sense if the entire sentence is a question.
The speaker speaks to an unknown listener.
Inference could mean two things, and the season
is over, so you just have to start over.

The secret police. The Right is wrong.
Finally, a clue is given. The clue is that
there is a listener.

Her outsider position/my insider position. Her insider position/
my outsider position.

Don't take measurements of the situation, of life,
comparisons. Just look at ewe and prunes; keep using
semicolons, it never ends, but it sort of does.

G., in a dress, premonitions, with the TV's ions.
The power of "the distance of the distance" is a temporality.
Owl on the dancefloor. "The incomprehensible messages
of tree-frogs." My attitude makes sense in context.

Nomadically following the buffalo//our art form.

A memory of an early apprenticeship.
The "land catching up to me," as if I'm running from it.
Something noticed at the start. New to sequins,
new to the land, new to having it all wrong.

The noble experiment, changing your plans,
canceling good health, a diversion.
That one step into harmlessness.
Poignancy paid for, the outrider, the rigged deal.

I keep finding typos everywhere in multiple books I'm reading.

Transitive verb without its object, hovering
in the air like an unstated, temporary solution.

"Less Hygiene, But More Spirit"

A new introduction, although everything
's been introduced already.
Incidental gentlemen of impartiality.
A list of singularities you don't believe in.

But the contaminated area is where we live.

Laws for swans.
This section is written in a persona.
Coming to understand the context you're living in,
and then suddenly it changes.

Less aware of the other chair,
and how close or far away
from despair you are.

In the morning, waiting for an introduction
that is an extrication. Circumstances
as a form of slough.

A list of things that are one thing, but that are also a set.
Then a list of things that are one thing, but singular.
A "craft" or a "bourne."

The aesthetic experience of being with friends,
losing everything that feels like joy in my cells,
to be replaced with vague aesthetic pleasure.

The spot, where we live, to avoid, of contamination.

A list of things or people or consciousnesses
that could have "bluster."

[Cute barista: Grey long-sleeved shirt under black and white horizontal striped short-sleeved shirt tucked into jeans with a belt, tapered frayed legs and ankle boots.]

A pronoun that replaces a situation.

Turning away from delusion.
Some connections are just a moment of looking up.
Taste of papadum still in my mouth.

The repeating red X. Marthe's red X.

Not knowing whose house you're staying at.
List of conversations that you wish you didn't have to hear.
The plot marginal to the explanation of it.

Rhianna and Drake vs Gordon Comstock:
Work, work, work, work, work, work //Money, money, all is money!

“Back to the Dollhouse”

The new narrator is female, and she starts in medias res.

We know where it starts but not sure where it ends.
This section begins with a “we” that is either including
the audience or including the previous narrator.

Pray-painted, or spray-painted.

A tension that needs to be worked out
through extreme movement
or physically scribbling words incessantly.

Harmony, something across from you that can be addressed.
Or something you are within, that surrounds, a peace.

An interjection that “there is more”
before there was an intimation
that anything had even occurred.

Not going exactly right. —George Bush on his first visit to the Gulf since Katrina

Quietly stewing in some threshold,
but leaning into some future moment
where the shade will not be so shady.

1. Literal event 2. metaphor 3. metaphor 4. simile 5. metaphor
6. metaphor.

The future, stepping toward you, eyeing you, interested.
Impregnation by a wick.

[I ask him what he’s wearing. He says a black shirt.
I ask him if he’s wearing pants. He says

Yes underpants. The text comes three times
by accident. Then he asks me if I'm wearing a dress,
but I'm not. I'm wearing yoga clothes.]

Ashbery's ambient "it." The it's anonymity.

Talking about the racism of the "savage" trope
And the history of the land means you have to say
"savage" and sometimes quote people who use the term.

"Primness of Outline"

The future's innuendo futile because itself's
self is choiceless. A list of choices during
indecision. Choices, the team colors; little vs small.

Polite savage with an easy manner.

Translation as a binary, and we understand
binaries as missing so much on the outside,
in between. A nonbinary translation
would be slightly outside of understanding.

The Audubon sequence.

Does the wick always have to be a candle,
time's representation? We are still in this place
of entering a threshold, or maybe we're just looking at it.

Standing, contemplation, the "primness of outline,"
a testimonial, time addressing itself next to you.
One's self becoming a metaphor for transportational
devices. A terminus.

How do "people" arrive inside the narration,
inside our narrator? As if this self is devoid of personhood
and is only some sort of technological device
that evolved to help others arrive/switch directions.

Being neutrally helpful.

Everyone who arrives, gives up.
When the narrator switches identities, we imagine
it might be momentary, but maybe it's forever.
Me, I, no one, no one, you. The narrator as ego.

But the land can't write.

That moment when first person slyly becomes second.
The I becomes a you who wonders about one's dream.

There is a wind, a platform, and pigeons,
but the metaphor might be so deep now
that there is no hope or possibility of the literal.

I think it's so wild to have two omniscient narrators in a poem.

“And the Woman with Orange Pink Hair Stood Silently By”

The explanation merely a device
that allows the narrative to continue,
but really the point is to continue.

The missing topiaries.

Once we’ve completed the misunderstanding.
Some magic that comes around and attempts
to announce some better civilization
that couldn’t possibly exist.

But magic itself a possibility that is not possible.
What a post-Wagnerian impressionistic world is,
would be. Rivers and dreams and stones and edges,
but with some sort of post-music component.

The affability of the supplicant. —Hejinian

The word “gare” in italics. Post-Wagnerian
as post-myth but also encapsulating myth.

“How am I supposed to know which/ ticket
goes with which entrance portal?”

Would the secondary narrator even discuss the mail
in her insistent explanation? The woman who
is explaining might have something to say
about a grievance form.

Infected with change, as if it’s some tool
they might use if they need it.

Gears, motors, a hunger, stalactitic dripping.
Negative capability's incapability.

The invisible breathing down your neck.
The invisible birthing the invisible
until it builds up and you trip over it.

What the landscape replaces.

Another famous composer intoned and we forget our scarves.
Nonsense's pattern. How alone urges you
into eye contact, or toward. Patterns, conditions
and probability. Meaningfullessness, living without,
or only on hold. That thing we're writing about's destiny.

"Elaborate charade" in quotes.
Doppelgänger without an umlaut,
a "lost bairn."

I still don't know which narrator is speaking.

“The Pugilists Have Returned to Their Corners”

Large space between questions about a stinky lagoon.

I don’t do “thinking” as a pursuit until I’m writing.
And once I stop, I forget. Steve wants to talk about
self-remembering. Ashbery wants to talk about destiny,
free will, predestination, self-determination.

Trash as armament, weaponry, rebellion. Eros(ion).

Allergic to your allergy.
He is starting the story over in a different way.
Biographical, controversial, a publication,
reference to teaching. Memories jumping
all over the timeline.

Using someone’s dishes in the employee kitchen,
and not knowing whose dishes you are using.

[Barista is asking a regular if he considers himself a regular.]
How often we tell our friends stories as parables,
to say what we cannot say.

The houseless’s lack of privacy, so they have to do everything
in public. Soap box with a joke. Not sure if I got that pun, in
the text. A viola, some ouzo. The 39 territorial states. The
junior ones, missing at some point, never appearing again.

[A guy is yelling very angrily at the barista,
because she won’t give him the wifi code,
which she won’t give him,
because last time he was watching porn.]

All history is palimpsestic.

Point of transition, reconsidering.
[Barista's dream recounted of seeing their teacher in their dream, but it is a clone teacher and they murder the clone.]

See the chance in the obscurity of chance.

“A Reworking, a Scissors-and-Paste/Job”

Bombast, hijinks, uproar.
Translation into dahlias, crocuses, cats.
“Durch ein ander” in italics.
The translation/transference confusing.

The unlawful law, self against self.

When it’s dark, it’s just dark.
The problem of difficult people
and how to process yourself in relation to them.
The extinct subspecies of us.

“Siding with the morally bankrupt.”
Talk to the dark about the time, about time, keep your
bearings. “Those who offer no moral incentive to cling
together.”

The slaves that belonged to convents, nunneries, monasteries.

Not aware of the moment when you left the narrative.
Identity is not the problem.
Holding on to the back-up plan in your back pocket
just in case. You can’t believe it until you smell it.

Pocket dial, pocket SOS. Mid-age,
the forest is behind you in the distance, but not yet
out of sight. A future history no one believes in.

One success leads to gambling for more.
A metaphor you need the biography to understand.
Pound telling H.D. not to go. Thwarting the future
inevitability, but the labyrinth only has one answer.

The words "beautiful" and "quiet" repeated over and over.

Another order told:

1) feather
2) dust
3) flourishes in a signature [after that], "with," "were," "and," and "the letter of personality lessons."

The explosion. The BP explosion.
Prefiguring what you died in the middle of.

A second quietism. [to insist on the letter]
[of] [personality lessons] To admit to a feeling.

Present mistake foreshadowing a future success.
Love letter to someone lost along the way.

“Dead End Near Where the Coats Were”

“A fertile monotony.”
The worldly they vs. the royal we,
“if it can be done, why do it” —Gertrude Stein

A mention of that which is a second story. Extremity’s relation
to a mind that thinks itself extreme.

The ecosystem’s vision expands to include us.

So, there is magic and there is a foreign language, there is
thought, but a vacuity within it, there is escape, possibility,
permission. The story is held in vacuum, not to be returned to.

The instability of every moment and every relief. Staying put
where you are and the anomalous moment, connected but improbable.

We are the problem. We are victims of the problem.

Obscuration, replication, the obsequious. Generational relief
of anxiety. Is the “we all,” just me, the royal we, or maybe
the friend I’m with.

To create a counterfeit of reality more real than reality.

The beginning is the end. And something ends.
A series of steps, an order to things as they happened.
We walk away unscathed, or at any rate, our wounds invisible.

Unexplained phenomenon.

Your death parallel to your birth.
Mistaken assumptions: The night is not the night.
There is a storm.

If the period is an epoch or an ending,
but either way rounded.

Architecture/cities appearing out of nowhere,
but somewhere, and with a volition and a velocity:
"a repertory of trees." The architecture not in conflict
with trees, but in concert with. The trees, the charmed,

sideways looks, colorful turns of meaning, a historian
or archivist taking notes to the side.

A map titled "Where Bodies Were Found."
A map titled "All Gabled Roofs Will Fail."

Looking again, but the notation
is made with invisible ink
never to appear a minute later.

Repeating the Oracle: "Repetition Makes Reputation"

This section is about beginnings.
But also returning,
which might be the same thing.

Maybe next spree. The full decade.
When you go out shopping next,
find us a different time to live in.

Academia a retreat and something to escape from.
Bastions of "why do I have to be sitting up,"
but this is something I've chosen, and so I will.
We are not birds. But they are:

Colonists like the other birds.

Pre-internet web written about in the internet age.
Breaking up the monotony with an intonation of song.
The fairytale as an intermission.

My age is a badge, so stop badgering.
Something highly irritating described
as "nice ambient music."

The End intercedes on our behalf,
and we can finally relax.
The natural world presents itself as if it's ours,
but somehow, we find nothing is ours.

Rumination just means you haven't written it down.

We don't consult oracles for accuracy,
but to be engaged with the self
and universe-interrogation.

Repeat what you want to believe
and not that that makes it come true.

h e m o r r h a g e s i n t o t h e G u l f

Materials as territory.
Make a vow.
The building beside that territory.

The blurred-out word merely a preposition.
In an older age when the new was newer.
Sustained unresolvability.

Yes underpants

Yes underpants

Yes underpants

"Clad in Dimity"

Things that didn't go nearly so wrong back then.
Dial-up's lamentation of time.
Imagination seeing the self, metaphor of the imagination,
using Carthage as its object.

The way Michael Cross corresponded with Scalapino for so
long that she corrected his misreadings of her, but I'll never
know my misreadings of Marthe.

"The possibility that a trick was involved."

Memories that themselves are in the past tense.
Underdog into the wolf.
The difference between "in" and "to" changes
the entire meaning of the previous verb.

reflection/crystal/dew/drop

The object of the metaphor
and the object that is the metaphor.

Imagination unbelieving, staring in the mirror
at what it is and what it is not.
It's not nothing.

empathy only gets us so far

It is at this point that some sort of angry cuss fit
seeps out onto the page, finally.

A boundary between
here and civility that is beyond
the boundary

and so we assume possibility
and choices
that we cannot quite see.

"See how it comes undone": it being the house, survival,
our days. Saved by a moment of sunlight, or that cloud,
or dogs. Gloriously/gloomily curtaining down,
living by wits/not staying in bed.

Gabriel Garcia Marquez's cursed town.

The Sky is Falling
The Walls Do Not Fall
All Gabled Roofs Will Fail

A list that is just titles of things.

Wits tell you everything unbalanced is hanging in balance.
A list of reasons that are not the reasons why I love you.

III. Poetry's Anti-Monument

"The Usufruct of the Sparse"

Mythology but not a particular one.

"The day of doom universally misconstrued
as a time of relief."

An occasional I, an occasional him.

"I was depressed when I wrote that. Don't read it."

What sleep is.
As if memory must be renounced.

Reading about ecomimesis after having dreamed
about going to a museum of the DFW airport
that was a replica of the actual DFW airport
item by item, and wondering if this was a dream
of a simulacra, and why would I dream this?

Post-millenarian tintinnabulations.

Then a list.

A memory of the mis-
step is not as bad as the misstep
at the actual moment it happened.

Narrative story as just another fragment of the collage.

We are always trying to replicate ourselves
to save ourselves from extinction.

Your rival, your double.

"Just be calm, don't/rush, it's all over soon."
Reorganizing irregularities. What is hidden's
explication. "Roulades" in italics.

Huge issues of the day casually alluded to.
The future's recognition of the lie, obscured.
The religious host needs a religious parasite.
It's easier to cut than to fill in.

That we could capture the other
on the page, through art, and thus dominate it,
but we don't realize the other is ourselves, and so
we are only dominating ourselves.

[the sadness no one will recognize]

Poetry that's undermining poetry
's anti-monument.

“Particles Turn Nasty”

The popular screening out the real.
A reconstruction of the lost that would be a falsification.
Because what is lost is crossed out,
so no opposition is seen.
How chiaroscuro shows what is
by highlighting what is not.

I actually marked where I stopped reading in the text,
having been slowly, yet spontaneously interrupted.

Going to the island to read books of the history
of the island.

To distill the few things that happened
into some sort of autobiography, into
a worthwhile reduction. Leaving behind
this reduced distillation in some sort of unclear rush.

An explanation surrounded by semicolons
that is no explanation.

Recreating what you’ve rejected’s failure.
Saving what was lost and what we’ve refused
to recreate as something in your mind.

Since the war the ocean reclaimed its own.

When it feels like reality is completely working
against you. Subordinating conjunction that means
in addition to.

After asking this question, you are clear
-ly crossing the street and nearly getting

hit lost in thought. Then suddenly
using science as a metaphor.

Particles, a diagram, subsistence.

"It Seems I Can't Think" Either, John

In addition to reality falling apart,
"the other is there," convulsive
happiness, left with darkness.

But maybe this other is not the comforting other,
but the other that is also turning nasty along with
the particles.

Third choice, best choice:
the other as an adjective with a missing noun.
Paralysis because of the missing _______
and some other other messing with the particles.

Marthe researching in the library on the Island,
two hours away: "white," "octaroon," and "colored"
head the list of women's names.

The fullness is only a map of what once was
and all is lost through the turning/change
of particles. The other there like a ghost
suffocating the we, hovering over.

What would make more sense in contrast.

The thing that is a memory of what no longer is.
A relation between things that are still there
but the things themselves are not.

Just looking for scraps on the floor.

Presences amongst trees, able to be received.
A sexual metaphor insinuating one of violence and rape,

but this is about something mystical, about trees.
Now we know who the other is.

The other is you, yourself.

The invisible city inside the storied one.

1) You could buy quantities
2) leave them in your yard
3) mix with others.

After the colon, a list of animals, to contradict
the plants or continuing along in a similar vein.
The connection between the disparate told:
"abrupt elements in the sun."

"Abrupt Elements in the Sun"

The relief an irruption.

This might be for me like that dream I had once:
One of my many childhood heaven dreams
that the memory of would greatly calm me
and even be some sort of safe space, yet now
I think of it and cannot regain that feeling
of relief, but can remember it.

Realizing the second person must be the husband.
Having no parallel experience of "you."
Facts without politics.
"Yet" substituted for "if."

Names retained by the cartographers.

As if this relief could be some sort of entity
that could turn to you. A different turning
than the way the particles turn. Rebuilding
our wall as something crumbled that you
are rebuilding.

The missing parts in the diagram we remember,
but are gone.

A verdict in which one could possibly be forgiven.
The other, the husband, leaving before the trial
was finished, as it would be too "confusing and painful"
to the house/their house.

Neither of this place nor entirely alien to it.

The verdict, to the other that is not the self,
but an actual other (or maybe the self's self)
is excusable. The word that is that word,
some bandied about, meaningful word
that becomes a point of contention.

The wakeful are embarrassed by the (embrace of) sleeping. —Hejinian

A moment away from abstractions.
Mundane events like going to a shopping mall, kids,
houseplants.

The one being unsure about something that the other
(implication) is sure about.
The mottled sold to the albert.

“The Edge of a Cross-Section”

How you must accept the mundanities
that in their plurality become a sum
greater than their parts, unless
you want to become the less valuable one
you were while in the mundanities of parts.

Listening leads to lists.

The thing that will come around, that always comes
around, but that hasn’t come around yet, and is still
too early for.

Concentrated disadvantage and homicide rate coincidence.

Your retail version that wants to step away from itself,
but that action would keep you in partiality. So, you skip
instead towards the sum of the memory, where the manual,
manure, anti-social, and anti-aesthetic thoughts all come together.

This is a really good topic to address in the story of a life.

They can understand each other
in the graphical D-6ian grid. Some sort of
seasonal infrastructure that is raised
for some sort of seasonal yearly occasion.

Salinity management vs restoration

Can they all understand X ,Y, & Z even though X & Y are highly complex
and A, B & C are not used to thinking in this way?

The project parallel with an occasion it’s too early for,
but being compelled to continue on even though
the parallel is not yet parallel.

“The Man that I Entered”

What I cannot parse and if it will make sense later.

“How idle folks get well off,”
and we remember our forgiven
poverty. The memory or fact of this knowing
a place for only “thieves and innocent children.”

“The rust-colored lots…
like the one where Mercury slew Argus.”
Trickle of associations. The story of youth
or a memory associated with,
then associated with mythology.

Tricked into trickery
to hide one shame or other.
Predictions by the moon.
What crops there will be,
what we’ll receive, what we won’t.

Marthe Reed After reading your response,
it is obvious that you have an agenda.

“But go on” you, listener,
leave the space of this story,
while I part ways with all our mythologies
for work, the employer, the place of employment.

Dry and tidy’s space has to be entered
to reenter the wet field.
Going to the desolate
to avoid being sent to the desolate.

He's writing about something that used to happen
and still does, that he's come back for,
yet he can't get the project going. Whilst that inability
to get the project going is the project.

Second clause that might be an answer to the first,
or just a second thing in a list. As if a caress could be
something that could be opened like any oyster.

“Baffled by a Sandstorm”

Not realizing, until I reached the seventh clause,
that this was a question.

Being nonintuitive is a sort of asshole move.
A kink that is always wanting one more thing.

Snakes in the crotches of trees.

The beauty hidden in time.
Made into imagery.
That second type of intelligence.

That which is just energy
without any cerebral intent or knowledge.
Pencils as a sort of fermata.
Waiting until that moment when the again happens.
Cats, wild animals, python’s emergence.

What we’re taught about the night
and how we are to occupy it. [Arced cloud.]
Forwarded application as a metaphor for life.
Then some biblicality.

The document stated that they would leave the country
before they would sign an unconditional oath.

Because the future is a dead end.

Missing out on what you’re growing out of.
The reality, in real life, so much more interesting
than the report back.

One of the popular ones who seem blessed
and charmed but don't know how they did it.

Our memory has a context,
a choir,
are the many-voiced,
ending with implication.
This is a telephone call.

Rereading the sentence to find the question.
The bird's song is not an attack.

That which gives an unimagined affluence
destroys the landscape upon which their identity hinges.

Just appropriate the dead and you'll be fine.

"A Primary Mood of Spells and Rituals"

The question starts with a question.
Our knowledge is not authority.
Our knowledge is in community.

Justification of seasons.
A summary of the summery.
The understandable problems, troubles, cases
presented, orderly-like, but then getting out of hand.

Momentarily appearing.
Smell the air for what's coming, then hide again.
The impermanent permanent.

Winners of Louisiana's coastal disaster.

Shuffling the cards
as a metaphor for steadiness
within unsteadiness.

You don't want to end up merely in imagining
something. As if we're in some climax
that's important. The important thing
is rest and safety. The Golden Prize's
illusion in itself. The collapse's inevitability.

Magic in the night, trapped in our invisible powers.
Aversion, a step toward winning.
As if it's morning when it's not morning,
but the birds know what it is.

resilience practices

"Contemplating the sky from the other side."
The sky's warning stickers.
The void's void does not contain void.

The parallel's interchangeability, and
as if that's an error.

NOT: pernicious, tenuous, tenacious, perspicacity,
BUT precarious.

"Dull Plumage of Another Kind"

Hermitting from the top.

Endorsing something tame.
Generational grapplings with language's altercation.

zooming in to capture the finer details

Polished yet still irrelevant.
Not walking along with everyone else.
Feeling like you're halfway in
but discovering you're nowhere.

Invisible and it's a bad thing.

The Plot: Aging.
Writing longhand like writing onto wood.
An authority but without sense, not meaning dumb,
but inanimate.

the margin always in flux

Ashbery's own disestablishment.
Plumage around doors and windows,
not a material plumage, but psychological.

Isolation's center is always a building of some sort.
Multi-storied truth.

the names of lost bodies of water

Some of you will join me in my hermitude,
and some of you will not, but it won't matter so much.

The image of being so high above.
What matters and what does not.
Rational speech, the sun.
Variations like plumes.

“. . . In That Lurch Before One Sees”

Conjunction of addition
where you expect one of opposition.
What matters interrupts what is mattering.
Not able to answer but accidentally answering anyway.

The problem, the problems, the problematic
on the white board, solved, but not erased
and the solution untenable, unwritable, ineffable,
but effable to some.

There’s a lot of shouting in this part.
An immunity that never comes.
Pleading into ellipsis . . .

§

I want a pendant of the Section Mark sign.

There is violence, but it is somehow in the distance,
doesn’t encroach, but is ambience dampened,
and everyone feels their party was ruined,
but not everyone. Not everyone was having a party.

Some were sad in their rooms alone,
having panic attacks. Others in the shadows.
Desire like an inconceivability.

Shadows holding them back,

restraint of shadow
holding down shadow
hides from shadow
in the shadow.

Or the changing light and how it hurts you.
Walking home, then being at home.
The safety of home's impermanence
and the awareness of it in increments.

Identifying harm through the tracing of lines on a map.

“Harvest as an Adjective”

Spring’s arsenal.
We know what that means.
As if we’re collecting telescopes.
Hoarding stars.

Truth backs up against the wall.
Charm’s enemy with such a straight back.
Precious, bread, weeping, the cross, “nice,” lurching.

Agricultural nitrogen
Agricultural phosphorous

One moment in the midst of religion, its closed system.
The weather is not like it used to be.
Always sitting in the darkest place in the café.

That moment when it’s too late for memories
is not a moment I’ve yet experienced.
The moment that is too good to be followed into
is also so because it is too late.

The way pagan cultures accepted the new religion
by Christianity’s repeating & emphasizing the symbolism
of the Mother, the oil business replicates aspects of
a fishing culture through proximity to and livelihoods of
the water.

No one is left, or no one dares
to step into that timespace.
If you are not asking the right question,
it makes you into a type of liar.
Like sidestepping the situation.

How is the weather? It's colder. It's still raining.
Some of us have to be liars to make truth mean
something, maybe soon none of us will have to be liars.

[I have so many male platonic friendships right now.]

He wants to know about the dark side,
questioning the religious question.
What you've avoided all your life, at some point
becoming curious.

“The Harvest Home Had No Walls at All”

What was home is no longer. This wall-less
home & this non-home home, is a harvest because
the absence is some sort of beginning.

Corn grew dear. —Joanna Southcott, 1794

At the corner is not the same thing as cornered.
Every occasion leaving uplifted and hopeful in
the midst of emptiness. The four horsemen.

These tears that cover everything.
A possible confrontation but it evades the situation.
Confrontation’s possibility.

We want to be faced with ourselves
but are faced with profiles
looking away, off in the distance.

hyacinth-and-lotus / ((hallucinatory /
(body))) / garden ::

Keeping the distance between us all a thing.
But stepping out of that/this blurred distance
would also be not a solution.

Let the situation figure itself out.
Is it the human condition to be ________.

Homer is dreamless. —Hejinian

“Reading, Apparently”

Back to what I was saying.
Casual quiddity.
An ox’s neck means this setting is rural.

There is a “he” and he “came at” our narrator.
The next sentence is about time.

matter d i l a t e s

Spars of flame, burning grass, a joke though.
Not like the rapture, a mundane moment
with elements of apocalypse. The old traditional
ways making contact with revolutionary ones.
But just small little moments, “nodules.”

The methodical’s wild underbelly
exploding in our faces.
Ashbery’s cyborg imagery.
Just another pastoral metaphor.

Old men protected by a slow voice, speaking softly,
asking questions as statements. The introverted “sick
behemoth” wanting to go to the birthday party.

My Audience Is the Future

Reference the present.
The smallest possible bucket.
Future-proof.
Hypothetical triangulation.
Now so skeptical.
Subtle nudge from the programming librarian.
Historical data is useful.

Delve into your data.
Segmenting your audience.

Disobey authority —Alice Notley,
but also "authority" outside, reading
on their breaks, in stolen moments.

Searching the grass for abstractions,
predictions for the future.
Skeletons standing around under umbrellas,
until you start the work and they go back inside.

“Periods of Ritual Slump”

After the cyborg imagery, pre-Obama drones.
But it might just be a sound.
As if a sound, or music has a personal self, a conviction.
The sound as possibility.
Even the first possibility.
The drone’s later staged tirade, closed to.

“The sudden unnatural brightness.”
The reason we all see a light when we’re dying.
You’re in the last stage.
[The only reason I like this hip-hop song
is because he says “vintage.”]

Someone moved the swamp.

Thinking if this happens a second time, I’ll die,
but then it does, and then goosebumps, & bliss.

Death’s inauguration brought by a delegation
of children uninterrupted by the plans of bureaucrats.

They who thank you for the nightmare.
The nightmare you enter into
that frees the next generation from having to have it.

Hybrid realm, wet and dry, woods and fields

Language is a living being and doesn’t always
obey the rules that it’s supposed to.

“Never mind that it’s too shrill
for some ears to pick up on.”

As if you meant to do it this way all along.

Legalese turns the corner and becomes theological.
Original sin/ “original dignity.” Besides X, or Y.
Antiquated career-choices that now seem magical.

“And the Sad Birds Walked Away”

A circus, witness, spectators, the other team,
“Song like fire,” not the hustle, but hustled.

“Simple lives were also led.”

A perpetual crescendo that never reaches a climax.
A crescendo of feeling, not of sound.

The evening so pure it is like sex.
The evening and the fabric, one.
Both sometimes buried.
Sometimes you have to be loud.
A thought or experience as something to come back to.

And a love of porch music.

It might be something almost technologically Cyborgian,
but not with an implication of plastic or metal
hardware, because only in the mind.

And those other times when sex has nothing to do with it.

Song as a location.
The “it” and the “this,” poetry,
as often as possible.
Everything is up for discussion.

Sex like writing, similar in that some surprise
happens and you never know what’s going
to happen until it comes out of you.

Sex like a “quiet corner of a garden.”
TMW not a threat but a greeting.

Before relating a mundane activity,
short musing about the writing process.
A range of hilltops to look from.

“Calm Self-Esteem”/“Neutral Benevolence”

Musings that masquerade
as mundane activity descriptions.
Intoning oxen as a metaphor for truth.
They watch everything we do, even our dreams.

Returning in the evening with no resistance,
maybe we are the ones watching x happen,
and just as we watch the x that happens,
we watch it dissolve in our memory.

“extractive detritus/sparkles invisibly from its depths”

Wondering if these rituals are pointless.
Same sort of wondering about what my own life means
where you make some sort of sad statement
about how dire your life is, then you say “unless,”
“mere symmetry is death.”

We’re in the Calvinist section.
“Imparting goodness to the coils
of superstitious industriousness.”

The truth of work when it comes out
of the depths of your soul. The rewards
of whatever, just passing by. The reward
is not the reward.

Nine minutes of throat dub.
Before the repetitiveness becomes repetitive.
Let’s just keep the myth of the day right here,
unexploded.

Marthe Reed's answers
to Bhanu Kapil's questions for nomads.

Ridiculousness a topic of what we don't care about.
This is the section about bunnies.
"A feline quickness and fur."
The outside other's interposition.
The fatal gradient.

A drone that is not a drone, with beats, but the beats
become sort of dronelike after a while.
The outside other's interposition.
"...and in that moment I saw myself
on a visit to myself."

“Crags and Castles and Honeycombed Grottoes”

This part is about identity and multiplicity.
One self against the other.
We love it when the other identities recede.

Just what you pass on the way to wherever
small talk in the dusk. The self’s unfamiliarity
with the self. Random nature imagery ending
in “Hesperides.”

an effort to remain in place

As if the self doesn’t belong to the self
but to someone else. Breaking your associations
which will also work. Impulse ≠ Sincerity.
The sure places necessity.

Preparing for dwelling in it, preparing to dwell
but this is not a home, a space for living.
Maybe a space to die in.

UPDATE: no additional information.

Walks of sand.
But make sure there are paths in and out of the space
like the space is a brain,
but a brain you want to get free of occasionally.

Leslie Scalapino writing about pears.

[Purple weather, purple writing, purple film,
my purple novel. But poetry is not
this dwelling, death space, rumination brain.]

No observable/trees

Poetry as minutia. The moment, sounds listening,
godless not in reaction, but godless in subtraction.
Recording effort.

Cats finding a better spot.

"Some whitecap curdles/ in a leaden expanse of water
and we are aware this moment/ has done its share,
that we shall not be needing this batch of insight again."

Writing as a question you wonder about vs
writing as a question writing insists on asking you.
Trials related to writing written in the future perfect tense.

"With Stone Lotuses and Iron Epaulets"

Us, the ones forgotten, unnoticed,
the group of us that receives no hype,
no one wonders what we're up to
unless they're making conversation.

But the other of us seen as hipster, materialist,
populist, just pulling a scam. And in between
the two leaders as ghosts. But anyway, move
aside for the next big thing.

certain seismic /real-time data

I always felt like I'm in a space between two different
life phases or in between different groups of people
and there's no actual group for people like me,
"as in a quarry where no breeze stirs."

The scarcity of where/how to find your voice, your flow.
And you just sit there waiting.

Artemisa absinthe blue blue

The self not quite right
and even your looming demise will not correct it.
The time wrong, longing for something other,
but having to work into or work out where/
when you are.

This is somewhat related to the text
because he says "delicious paradoxes."

((fennel/ day shimmering

This is Ashbery's anime section.
Omniscient cartoon watcher.

[Seeing a woman get in her car,
then reading for a while,
and after I look back up again,
surprised by the presence of a different car.]

What you know for not having researched it.
The magic comes as un-real-ity, a materialization,
dots join, a whirlwind that "vaporizes moods,"
and an astrologer.

"It's a River and One Must Keep Up with It"

If you could live fully aware of all the things
that others are jealous of you for.

Revelation against the stars decree.
The error on a doorstep, waiting for economics
to supervene this undue patience.

A word that is both a word and not a word.
I know when you do your homework, you're angry.
Everything's gone wrong because I changed my writing ritual.

bruised awake

Tragus piercing. Everything you do instead of writing
hurts you. Everything always works out, but just barely.

[Can I just get the English muffin?]

Childhood narrative as metaphor for wherever you are
at some point as an adult. Feel out others and decide,
step out of the fermata void. Chaos magic. Maybe
you just want chaos.

The weather, natural forces, the engine's desire
taking you away from this thing that you want.

As if the fermata gets pushed into another from Oz,
something more mundane, but with no noticeable
difference, or epiphany. As if it were just another delay.
A delay that is not spiritual, but you come back with
the change as having missed the moment.

Loss as a vacancy.

Everything changed, no one admitting it.
Powerless to clean yourself, you must be cleaned.
Powerless to affect the change you want.

The use of someone more in pain than you are
as a device, to show the shadow side, and how
you are a voyeur of your shadow side.

Pure desire, purity of desire, inseparably linked
to one's own voyeurism of the self.

Oxymoronic conscientious voyeur
Oxymoronic conscience voyeur
Oxymoronic conscious voyeur
Moral voyeur/split life.

Language excerpted from language excerpted.

If you are doing this immoral thing
but fully conscious of a morality,
you will feel split
and perhaps try to cover your tracks
by using archaic language.

Saying "lemon" but meaning sex.

“But That’s a Small Cataclysm in a Landscape Now/ That’s No Matter”

Partially numb but music giving it back to you.
Wait John, how do you even know this word?

When you’re just drifting so nothing can happen,
nothing momentous, maybe nothing terrifying either.

The of and the about

What seems an obvious typo, meaning both words.
Not a space, but a major indentation. Inference
of exercise. Must be the 1980s. If “Shining Eyes”
is a reference to “The Stars Were Shining” era.

But we are not getting any exercise.
Past conditional. All regretting the lack
of exercise, living what you’d written
would have made it not necessary to write.

Some obscure, unfulfilled promise.
Either thing that could have happened, but that didn’t
was another condition that was also unfulfilled.

The result hanging in the ethers
....like eggs on the ground. Buds
that never grow and waiting and waiting
after having planted it. Capitalist functioning
without time as if outside of time, but merely time
hidden.

We are a hive.

A small cataclysm, a landscape, something perky
or melodic, irritation without discomfort. Failures
matter less and less, then at some point you stop
thinking even of yourself.

The hermitage reflex.
Melodies within loneliness.
A darkling making a cure.
Out of the flows, the circuitry, a curious entity
falls out of some dark ark.

Everywhere in the future
clearly only death and despair,
but for now a small lit place.

Then after a while,
there is more light
than is at first evident
in the space
you are occupying.

IV. The Flow of the Poem's Display of Itself

Even the Diabolical Orgiast Has Ascetic Aspects —Antonin Artaud

Predetermined seaweed.
A nature metaphor standing in for something natural.
A strand, the weather, pebbles, the undertow, eternal undertow,
in fact, seaweed,
some houses up the street.

That which appears temporary,
but turns out to be eternal.

That minute when you step out of your emotion
and think you see pavement in the distance
and the weeds you're slugging through
are thinning out and maybe there's a dirt road.

On this page, Ashbery is 59 years old
and has finally become conscious enough
to have his first nightmare, which is refreshing.

Enjoying the ordinariness of normal spats
or taking sides against someone.
Something others can be compliant with.

A woman or at least a female character, or at least the pronoun she.
Could be the wind for all I know.

Or, maybe not *slogan* as something you fall victim to,
but a way of collecting people
who are already thinking along the same lines.
The plot merely a pretext for description.

"Ambiguity Seems to Be the Same Thing as Happiness"

The undertow not intended to be dispersing.
Strange synchronicity that seems to be not
my doing in any way, but which seems to be showing itself
to me, and I don't know what to think.

A casual comment about the show.
Writing against/with/toward/about what you're reading
vs. reading as a background for what you're writing
that sometimes retracts further away and sometimes doesn't.

The shores' truth of itself extending further and further in view.
                    Coming to an agreement
as a sequel. Songs never end, they just vibrate off each other,
                                        resounding back and forth forever.
Half full/half empty, but about the shore.

So there's a woman calling over her shoulder
as personification of the riddle. A miracle,
a darkness, but a twilight.

A crest within silence. "O we were never a couple,
but"... Lantern-light, horn of distress, a perpetrator.
The thief's great outfit, sprawling, so we can see.
The truth as something not evident until you rush inside.

The wall and the stain in conversation seducing the rubble.
"And veiled day paled."   This feeling, inappropriate to who
we were, and only arising because of the question.
Coming back and coming back again.

"The Old Bomb Was Having Its Say."

In the new section, "he was still at it."
I assume either writing or sex.
All this through a sickness, despite it,
and blessedly because of it.

Hiding the subject matter and writing around it.
The lie we tell "for weren't we all equals under the law."
The excuse for unethical behavior "never my strong suit."

Not a hard worker, but calling the shots, referee,
"too much isn't enough." Telling yourself to feel it
less, or perhaps when what you've succeeded at,
is a fabrication, "a series of studies," alchemical.

This alchemy led to this, yes, but also
an inability to do basic tasks,
and an ego vulnerability
in no way necessary to life.

Critique of the critic   not doing the work
            it takes to follow,
that which is "painstakingly elaborated."

One's own regret over evaluating one's own poems.
The imagined offense of scientifically evaluating your own poems.

"A palace of mendacious rêves."

The poem masquerading as norm core,
but when you look inside,
"a profusion of ornament."

Ashbery so "confused" about the (to him) difficult modernists.

Illegal statements about youth.
Slow-paced remembrances.
Or parallel notations
that will offend the other party.

Your youth is not my youth,   so youth
                              is something with a wall around it.

"Personal-Pronoun Lapses"

The theme of this section is weariness.
A discussion of one's eccentricity.
Slight egocentricism and silent resentment.

The cozy bed, a proletarian, back breaking toil.
Discounting resentment with pretension.

There is a "he" and he is a child.
And he is responsible for technological
inventions of the future, which is now,
so our present present, in this scene,
is the past, the late mention of devices.

"in traces of the slightly altered climate
and the disproportionately enormous effect
it has had/on geography, roads and productivity."

The effects of his dreaming in open cornfields.
The problem of petty distractions
and following them instead of one's "bent."

Your bent also afraid to follow you.

But "he" is connected to sailing, is on a ship,
or a poop deck at the very least.

Sad about passions' short-lived moment and only if the time is right.
And how rare that the time is right.

There's no truth and understanding, just superficial trash thinking.
Another biographically unclear drama about canceled class,
canceled out of spite, "Whose? His or the provosts?"

A list of things/activities indicating giving up.
An atmosphere just as thick, but slightly lighter.
Witnesses "dragged in to recant," Marsha's baby,
party streamers, the question of mussels,   and a long
            quote from "Cedric."

The secretive others, keeping mum about it all.
"What could we have done?"
Malone's generalized imposition of "elegancy."

“The Japes of Skeptics”

Temperaments matched to eras and how what’s in style then
seems stuffy and so unpopular now.
One’s forgotten resolve in the moment.

There is no act of divination available to us, not even charlatans.

We can imagine how we are to blame,
but cannot state for sure. Norwegian
classical (playing)... Still patiently waiting
for peace and dignity. Maybe it’s only
the waiting
that brings it. The entertaining
point taking away
the truth from the truth.
His usual witty offset of the idiom left off
and just the idiom remains, revealing nothing but cliché
or revealing the truth of the cliché.

The shape of water—the princess without voice,
boiling eggs, looking at a scar, getting a timer
getting in the bathtub. Fine in the chocolate factory.
Timecards, so like in another earlier time.
They are janitors, in a science facility.
They are in Sector T-4. Something is howling
in the tonic they just rolled in.

Tantalus ⇝ tantalizing.
Password, ignored,
discarded the power hungry
as a plot device,
not an actual philosophical issue.

This is a weird movie. —my mom
Follow the protocol.

A mirror that is also a map.
What is hard is easier than what's easy
because what's hard is what we practice the most.
Latte after seafood.

"Something Sweet, Turning Over, Something Unbuttoned"

The colors in the dark.
Colors are memories.
Electric and hectic colors that are memories.

Where we are, there is wheat. All I can give you
is this memory of wheat and a robin.
"You have something new/that was not in the catalog I have."

A believer in the future but also
we can't stay in the sun too long,
but want to go inside
dreaming of the possibility
of what is happening outside.

Pre-Olympian/pre-Martian (cf. Hejinians' *Tribunal*).
Something that seems like a nostalgia so intensely
but it's nothing like any original: a copy of nothing.

"What color is to a colorless surface,"
which is its own type of endlessness
you get to glimpse only once.

Politicless early life politics,
an anger at being placed
in a bucket that you don't understand.

Mixing biblical metaphors with memories of your youth.
What is Canaan in the Ashbery mythology and why does it seem
it was high up like in a mountain and you had to descend down to it?

"A Distant Sister Comes"

Distant is unknown, unseen.
Something in the mist of our minds.
Literary analysis of your juvenilia.

Ashbery isn't actually difficult. He is, but all he's doing
is obscuring who and what he's talking about.
It's not actually difficult if those subjects were there,
so his difficulty is a trick.

Maybe all difficulty is a trick.

Letting go is the way to go
after the depression
when you realize
you'll never get what you want.
Pensive afteredness.

I think one might just as well pretend
that he is the center of what he's doing and what his experience is
and that it's only he who can do it. —Jasper Johns

Tutoring Spring Quarter day 1, 2018.
An older man from Iran wants conversation practice
and he has a topic. The topic is bosses.

Is it true, because it seems true, he says,
that bosses have all the power
and everyone does just anything they say.
So we talk about different jobs and different boss personality types.
It seems confusing what he is trying to find out,
but finally I ask him if it's different in his country
and he says no it's the same,
but he thought Americans would be more free.

“Like Sleepwalkers Amid the Gaiety”

Disasters float by, but not too closely.
Understaffed means someone is under or un-
employed. “Time,” which is in the past, cave walls,
a 3 year old’s wall, every unconscious.

Health is a heresy of time. Health means
you can work, but not this work, that other work imposed.

The theme of seasons and are we in our season or not,
but never while watching everyone else catching seasons.
We can’t reclaim our bodies as they were
but we can sing, and we have music.

Meat, food, ready.
Your crown is waiting.
Must be nice.
And that’s when you “pull the ladder up,”
so that’s why others of us don’t chase success.

The theme is some sort of literary catastrophe.
A duel, blown out of context, media silence.
Unclear why, but it had to do with time.
In another “time,” another decade, it
would never have happened.

“Sent off to the hills” to recuperate. The saturated sky,
an image not beautiful, an image of war. All the misery
tightly ravelled, little hope for loosening.

If you want to know Ashbery’s solution to all your pain,
it is “atmospheres and easy repose.”

“. . . and so History Constantly Dwindles”

The historian’s opinion is that this decade is the most decadent so far.
What we consume’s not meant to be consumed.
It’s meant to be looked at.

“That anyone should have to die” for us, but the sentiment left incomplete.
“Frank O’Hara’s poetry has no program and therefore cannot be joined.”

To ignore the establishment’s right to exist.
To ignore the rules of poetry.
No message beyond “this is me and I’m poetry.”

Because poetry by itself is never enough—
“a dish without a sauce,” critique of poetry society’s
wishes. “Not just Breton’s rodomontades.”

Being asked to explain a poem is like being asked to explain an explanation.
“The Stein-Toklas salon was a coven of Satanist Bolsheviks.”

Ashbery’s view that giving poetry readings was a fad.

Writing for the drawer.
Structured awkwardness.

Whoever said that probably didn’t have a cake that killed people.

"The Title Always Wins"

Vanity's pardon. Cudgels for defense. A secret inclination
I won't tell even you. War's narrative that says you're alive
because of X as if thousands of boys were your Christ.

The secret that steps away and betrays you in the end. I think
this part betrays you in the end. I think this part
might be written in a snide voice maybe.

A promise you did not make but should have.
Student describing himself as numinous.

Those arts that are practiced in the darkness of the study. —Rousseau

My poetic process a gilding, Jay Defeo shaping, building the paint
on top of paint, but rococo placements of X, just on the side of a corner,
light glued on.

Whether this is a linear narrative memoir or seeps back and forth in
between times.

"Juggling priorities."

That moment when charm can contain you.
Redress, containment, impediment.

The Green that impedes, a metaphor for that thing
that happened, that always stops you from going forward.

General to specific analysis in which "in this case" it "went well."
A ship, like a light in the distance—a "guidepost."
The shiver beyond the solemn. (The light comes after the shiver.)
Knowing enough to be prepared doesn't necessarily prepare you.

"As Long as We're on This Planet the Thrill Never Ceases"

This generational rift that would mean nothing today,
or a different meme-rift would replace the rift of yesteryear.
Modern but with rural lapses.
Riled at what possesses us.
That it makes no difference to this or that slight irritation or problem.
The end we see for ourselves, "our fate and death as one."
Not believing the approaching glow.
We are in the corners de-conflagrating.
Shadow-like things we trip through, to and froing.
The particular prescription for misery,
and suspicion is good enough right now.

Advice from some master or other put into your poem uncited—
"Meanwhile, be one of those/ on whom nothing is lost."
[humble dragon pose]

Feeling he's being snide again. Is this the rapist's narrative,
but with sarcasm, so we know it's not him, but what he's
witnessed: "only a few more who need to be drugged or convinced."

Never enter the future's possibility.
Happiness as a passivity.
Deny at every turn the happiness that could be attained.
Yet death is there if you turn around, so we generally will not turn
around. "The grave, good face to austerity," seriousness of death.

Riffing off Pound, but saying I guess
if you're right and this is what we're doing,
then I guess this is what we're doing.

Reservations with the new generation's insistence on ________.
Where one is living, somewhere rural, or a village,

grateful for the quiet, but having preferred something else,
while still recognizing the importance of gratitude.

"The question is not whether to proceed into the misunderstanding,
but how to extend the frame/more or less grouping us as we sat before."

"A Misleading Index of One's Intelligence"

Writing a lowercase b in cursive.
What if you were to make a roman numeral,
indented old school outline of your whole life,
and not miss anything.

It is desire and discipline, consistency
with both that yields the results
of the thing we want, and not giving up
even though hopeless and frustrated.

An ⤳ indentation. A reference to then,
so now must be now or closer to it.

Such a long sentence, you think you understand
what's going on, but then you keep reading and that's not it,
there's more to parse, and at that point you're lost.

What is suggested is that there can be two elements simultaneously.
And in this suggestion is the appearance of something real
that is not real, and this unreal thing is a "real element of choice,"
but is in hiding, hiding close near the root, near some beginning,
and this unreal thing is itself a metaphor of a sadness that is in shadow,
yet as a shadow everywhere and enormous.

To recognize the nature of a thing by outlining its parts —Barbara Tomash

Supporting point for a thesis about shadows.
Then grateful for, after shadowy similes and metaphors are stacked
up on top of other metaphors, a description of a very concrete problem
remembering a word. Or you can remember it in a foreign language,
but not in your mother tongue.

The Spartans were famously laconic, an adjective from the region Laconia.

The multilingual's ability to make themselves understood,
there is no underlying force of understanding, no "foundation/
that hope supplies when something is going well."

"The Glabrous Drop That Will Satiate Us"

The soul imperceptibly proportions itself to the objects that occupy it
—Rousseau

The cinnabar headlands
were maybe a convergence once,
but aren't now. So you won this,
but there are so many more winners
above you that your win goes unnoticed.

The "real fear where the story must be lived."
Watching ourselves as if we are not ourselves.
Observing through water, but not a metaphor,
but maybe actually a metaphor. The real nature
of the operation revealed.

Dream that if inside of privilege
could be revolution,
or that inside of privilege,
unseen, invisible, resides
a seed of revolution
to upend the privilege
it is housed in.

Walk out leaving your coat on the floor.

Spark. Powder. Blaze.
Sodium Silicate.

The moment between the cold and the fire.
How the [view] seems permanent,
until the moment when it wavers.
The "governor's trick," your confession,
constraint, exigence.

When will you tell me what I know you're doing,
that you've alluded to doing, that is something slightly different
but in a way where you can say, well that is what you meant.

Lying back down once you fully realize what you've done.

"Rejoice in the Exterior Outcome"

Poetry the only constant.

The best conversational style
is one that doesn't have a topic,
confetti in the cracks, should we
even pick it up, does it even matter.

Ashbery's political section.
Want it to be metaphoric, the "constituents,"
the art world, poetry gatekeepers.
They realize the poetry is beyond their understanding.
Don't fully realize his "darker purpose."

Being set free and being set free from fame.
Trying to remember in the sand what one's problem is,
clearly there is one, or many. An Emersonian reference.

How our connections diminish over time
"as long as everyone" keeps "silent."
A bargain too loosely agreed to
to be a bargain. "The landscape and hares,"
presentiment's knowledge of the future,
and now what might you say to me.

No parallel to my life.
Not being a public person.

My worry irrelevant to my identity,
and sorting out who I am, whichever,
whatever it is, and that "you'd" love me for it.

The ultimate identity is the two strands together.
Every heartbreak replaceable by another. The "you"

‘s generalization becomes anomaly,
or anomaly helps it become more specific.

A very, very long sentence basically about thinking.

"How All That Fluff Got Wedged in with the Diamonds in the Star Chamber"

As if this is a finality, but we know it's not.

This section is about reading that is compelling
and reading that is not so compelling.

"Dutiful Devotions:" 1) "Tangled Hope" 2) "The Proper Walk."

There is possibly still a visitor,
and definitely still a conversation.
But there are nurses here.
"We were talking about cats."
Having a cat and having a cat in a bag,
and not letting it out of the bag.
John Ashbery's helpful and unhelpful suggestions.

An amicable parting, but then no word.
What the news doesn't report.
Unclassifiable ghost.
Maybe the standoff is in our hearts.

All the things included in a report about an unidentified man.
Wanting to not really help someone who's kinda fucked you over,
but helping them anyway, maybe under duress.

An argument implicit in our very bones —H.D.

New monitors, a secular sermon, life advice, the sermon's pocket,
and that what is in it is a hurricane. The fight between us, in our bones.
Like H.D. and Freud. Like me and ____________.

"Gushing down on me like a bushel of affectionate children."
A little bit too much work that gushes down.

Demands on your time vs easy living.
Appearances and impressions, hard on the outside.
Can we speak about cats? And speak to one?

"What's Wrong with a Little Pudding?"

Setting: The prairie. Strategies for loneliness, disloyalty.
A birdcage, but this is not a concrete object.
Eternal peace vs tea parties.
Focusing down to the essentials. Still dizzy until spring is over.
Mist, pretzel sticks, a fancier existence.
"Love,/ The Human Pool Table."

The voice of the publisher.
I am sending you this email outside of the "I"
but maybe putting on a front of "I"
which is not usually or entirely the "I"
that that person might usually be residing in.

Jacaranda petals, as if that's something you could have.

Stepping back to look at the whole view,
but not seeing anything recognizable.
Everything analyzable, but shapeless images
that you cannot make anything out of,
unless you guess or superimpose
your own experiences onto the shapelessness.

Time shedding itself until there is nothing left.
But yet it never runs out. Was writing my poem
in prose so maybe Amy would like it, but I've gotten
tired of prose poems.

Partialities making up the wholeness of our experience,
but we never see the whole. Marketing strategy
made up through incorporating aesthetic theory.

Ashbery's "What's wrong with a little pudding?"
vs Eliot's Do I dare to eat a peach?

What you will do with your competitor in this atmosphere.
Shocked, but it's not real.
Avoiding absolutes, avoiding assumptions.
Putting in conditionals to avoid authoritarianism.
Shaking, falling down, eating lunch.
Not being really that attractive, but showing off your body anyway
because you know you're cool.

"No One Calls the Woman Who Walks Silently Away"

Seven clients but none of them able to identify what everyone else can
recognize.
The key to success withering away.
I'm really a glowing animal from another dimension.

The ways of meeting the oppressor so well organized.
Vermont or Asia?
My pathetic Crusoe.

Academic success:
Achievement Gap vs Opportunity Gap.
I will never have a spoon.
Waiting for the next one,
filling it up with writing.

Swaddled child fastened,
tied up as you tie up a horse,
as you lock your bike, getting by,
a pack-horse begging, a miserly,
mean, old odd man.

List of things I want to ask,
but when I see them they become irrelevant,
or sneak out in the awkwardest way.

I realize through tutoring that all the things
we think we're teaching through discussions and readings,
we haven't convinced them of and they are still just as sexist,
racist and homophobic as they were before,
but now they are having to say so explicitly.

Confrontation but with a cool breeze.
Giving up on taking notes.

The light like frost, collecting in crevices.
A mistake in perception.
A stain that is not a mirror.

Truth like a fold-out fan, and mine is right here.
My thesis on importance.

"It's My Sonata of Experience, and I Wrote It for You"

Chiasmatic jealousies.
Waiting for the mail, a phone call, the sun to rise,
time's cessation. The next frame.
I had a suburban childhood, not a pastoral childhood, like you.

Decisions lurking in the air, maybe the clock will strike 12,
but maybe it won't. Magic trick dreams are just one possible answer.
I don't understand compulsivity because I don't understand energy.
Imperious carport, my mute existence justified.

Poetry, yoga, meditation, reading,
texting with Cordelia, being in rooms,
cessation of thoughtforms: what is taking care
of me, in my convalescence.

The wisp of the wind around my skirt.
Sad in the absence, not of time, but time's
representative. My desire for gender abolition,
but my friend reminds me that some people
actually want to be a specific gender.

Leisurely lower middle-class existence.
A pillow and then spring, but written as a verb.
As if our forms, who we are in the world,
were sprawled contextually, but scrawled,
written down.

The outward behavior in a community,
behaving the way you were taught to.
Affection, a learned state.

The end moving further away from you,
instead of just stationary in the distance.

But now we return and so the end
is coming closer. As if revolution
is going in a circle, “and now we
have arrived at the place of resolution.”

"It Will Look Better on a Cassette"

Semicolons, 3
Colons, 8
Em-dash, 1

Depressed mundanity.

But in the middle of it or maybe because of it,
a passion, on your knees, in tears,
a secrecy or a privacy for it.

The songs are people, characters
created, placed, in certain areas.
The sonata, a manuscript.

Getting to the end and deciding to change everything you've done so far.

Distracted by crying or thoughts about crying
or the possibility of someone crying,
or the factual knowledge of someone's future tears.

But we don't carry around handkerchiefs.
Or: everything ends in dinner.
Or carnage.
Or this telephone call I'm avoiding.
Fate is fate because it's fate.
But maybe it's not: maybe there was a moment.

Or, a fulcrum in which everything could have changed.

“Each to His Own Bed”

The “d” elided. Disappeared.
What you look for to help someone,
forgetting the self, changing the whole plan.

Because someone sneezed,
I will be up all night.
If you plan your life to a T,
there is no room for the unexpected,
no room for “you”’s.

Polka dots at the funeral. Stream
of consciousness over streams
of consciousness. Chasing the flow
with another flow.

We (kill) die (each other) with orgasms or illness.
When fate changes and evolves so much,
it becomes something else, how can
it be fate? Mixtape of my life.

It’s over so I’ll see you later, or never.
Every project I’m working on
I’ve been working on for years,
and when people ask me what I’m working on,
it’s the same thing it’s always been.

The only thing real is beginnings,
which is a monument no one can destroy.
Clearly the beginning is the end
and this is the end of the stanza.
[   ]

The beginning's structure being built
while the power is out.
What is being constructed
is being changed
as it is being built.

“Not Quite Late-Twentieth-Century Panic”

The direction we aim our lives
without thinking
at war with the direction
we consciously aim our lives.

Living costs so much more as an adult.
Something building energetically,
and something that is a part of that
changing, and as it grows, some small aspect
of the thing being built also grows steadily.

The senses expanded to inner seeing in ultra violet. —Scalapino

Scenes and agendas
not quite interrupting
but like a diversion/spectacle to get distracted by
for a minute.

A low-key panic that wakes you up.
All of us, running out of the house,
at the last minute.

A metaphor too complicated to explain.
A difference that must be performed
but the othernesses appear exactly the same.

The provinciality of witnesses pulled along
with the witnessed into their own gravitied nostalgia.

The panic is not a panic if you don’t notice it.
Sleeping through the alarm clock.
When your problems mature faster than you do,
but their maturation is a weed.

"The eye in the church."

Not our vision becoming clearer,
but the abstract vision that watches us
opening its eye to see us, after a long slumber.

"A Doubt Hangs Like a Jewel"

Not doubt, but just a doubt, melancholy, itching your arm.
Before the Smashing Pumpkins' Melon Collie and the Infinite Sadness,
there was Ashbery's melancholy melon-colored doubt or
[abstract metaphor too complicated for an album title].

Remind me to remind you to leave me room for cream.
The doubt, our accuser, "pitting all that we said against us."

Just check the report.

A bunch of clauses leading to the same thing, that are all saying the same thing. I'm still not used to living, being in a body. Asking to be scorched, but then left, in flames. With the whole day in front of you.

Nothing to do with this passage but tweet it.
You will find me in my father's house, of blonds and lookouts over water.

4)The lighthouse, the warehouse—all of them in me, all of me in them.

All of you, all of you everywhere now.
He even brings up love, bluntly, just like that.
"But the police are everywhere."

Become what they are, the escape conviction.
Apology for drinking. Apology for drinks. Gatekeeper
kept out by the gatekeeper. Too much love for the immunological.

I want to invert her sentences to make them more concise.

Haste occurs [at] a murder [ ] because the person about
to commit the crime cannot stand surprise. —Hejinian

Plea for hats. Friendship. Beets.
"In the real world."
Some quotes are to be titles, some are to be narrative.

What is expected is the unsatisfactory,
unsatisfactorily in the air, landed.
Conjugate the air above us.

“Deceived in our Reckoning”

The devil’s reckoning, a deceit of deceit,
without us, we can’t take this on the bus.
My mother says what can you prove to me of memory.

Not at my level of happiness, what comes out comes out
so much harder. The salvage, all that’s left of our hopes.
Every translation an approximation. Every translation
generalizing vague-ifying.

5) What you put on with a different meaning.
What you put on for a different reason.
Walking around with this motto on my shirt.
To cave-in with respect. To cave-in unconsciously.
Waiting in line, looking at everyone not waiting.

6) Missing the Venganza, but here for the numbers.
Everything different and the community
collapsed, but in many ways still the same.

The coastline changes but is also always the same.
Everyone up in arms about how things have changed,
except for the new, who are delighted with how different
everything is here. You don’t put protective wrap on your dog.

The war between x and y.
The war that has always been, but ritualistically
as if the ritual protects everyone.

The war continuing, but the ritual taken away.
A kitchen table that evolved into grillwork.
What it’s like to be allergic to water.
When an explosion is not a death,
but a birth, a bursting forth.

"Mere Grace Notes in This Battle of Stupid Titans"

List of masculinist facts that are wrong.
How memory is one truth and two lies.

7) Suspended you have to leave/suspended
you can't go anywhere. Frustration like an aura
you can't step out of. What the silence does.
When you know where you want to go, and when
you don't know. I like the country, mountains, sky,
but I don't want to admit it.

The twerk, the curve, the libations.
The cow's brand. The tramp stamp.
The pig's tail, in the year it was cute.

Little dogs in arms. Exactly what was specified.
The meager, the bare, the trivial's embellishment.
Stupid moons. The Titanides. The parents of the Olympians.

Unutteringly useful feature. Amenities, amenable.
Pleasant things found to still exist after the plague.

Unfindability. Satisfaction. Appears.
What gift are you bringing? Afraid of fear. Of tomorrow.
Of stomach pain. Relax charmed heart it's over.
It's not over.

Everything predictive of the present moment.
We are quiet. Death is close by. And Emily is gone.
Ergo. Possibility or hesitancy. Doubt is the unknown
circling a fire.

The negative repeats, we cut it out.
It's still there, invisible grammar.

There is no flag. Speech act, an act of silence.
Nearness, proximity. What is this body of water called?
This is only an example.
"For" as a cause. Two prepositions in a row.
The opposite of an intervention.

Acknowledgments:

Thanks to Matina Stamatakis of *Human Repair Kit* for publishing some of these, in different form, to Sarah Mangold for publishing some of these (also in different form) in *Guest*, issue 6, to Malcolm Curtis of *Talking About Strawberries All of the Time*, to Sara Lefsyk of *Ethel Zine*, to Ann Pedone of *Antiphony*, to Rob Mclennan of *Touch the Donkey*, and to Jason Morris of *Big Bell* (issue 8).

The first section, here called "Richly Flows Contingency," was first published as a chapbook under the title *The Hyperobjective Marthe Reed* for *Dusie Kollektiv* 9, for the New Orleans Poetry Festival 2019, April 19-April 21, in honor of Marthe Reed.

All Gabled Roofs Will Fall was published as a chapbook from Smooth Friend in January, 2024.

Also thanks to Roof Books, Caleb Beckwith, Kate Robinson, to Brian Ang for including me in his "Assemblage Poetics" grouping, and many thanks to the writing group: Sarah Rosenthal, Mary Burger, Denise Newman, and Dana Teen Lomax.

the best in language since 1976

Recent & Selected Titles

- WINDOWS 85 by Chris Campanioni, 160 pp. $20
- BUMBLEBEES by Deborah Meadows, 100 pp. $20
- THROUGH A WINDOW by Norman Fischer, 104 pp. $20
- SECRET SOUNDS OF PONDS by David Rothenberg, 138 pp. $29.95
- HAND ME THE LIMITS by Ted Rees, 130 pp. $20
- TGIRL.JPG by Sol Cabrini, 138 pp. $29.95
- THE POLITICS OF HOPE (After the War): Selected and New Poems by Dubravka Djuric, Biljana D. Obradovic (translator), 248 pp. $25
- BAINBRIDGE ISLAND NOTEBOOK by Uche Nduka, 148 pp. $20
- MAMMAL by Richard Loranger, 128 pp. $20
- EXCURSIVE by Elizabeth Robinson, 140 pp. $20
- I, BOOMBOX by Robert Glück, 194 pp. $20
- FOR TRAPPED THINGS by Brian Kim Stefans, 138 pp. $20
- TRUE ACCOUNT OF TALKING TO THE 7 IN SUNNYSIDE by Paolo Javier, 192 pp. $20
- THE NIGHT BEFORE THE DAY ON WHICH by Jean Day, 118 pp. $20
- MINE ECLOGUE by Jacob Kahn, 104 pp. $20
- SCISSORWORK by Uche Nduka, 150 pp. $20
- THIEF OF HEARTS by Maxwell Owen Clark, 116 pp. $20
- DOG DAY ECONOMY by Ted Rees, 138 pp. $20
- THE NERVE EPISTLE by Sarah Riggs, 110 pp. $20
- QUANUNDRUM: [i will be your many angled thing] by Edwin Torres, 128 pp. $20
- FETAL POSITION by Holly Melgard, 110 pp. $20
- DEATH & DISASTER SERIES by Lonely Christopher, 192 pp. $20
- THE COMBUSTION CYCLE by Will Alexander, 614 pp. $25
- URBAN POETRY FROM CHINA editors Huang Fan and James Sherry, translation editor Daniel Tay, 412 pp. $25
- BIONIC COMMUNALITY by Brenda Iijima, 150 pp. $20

Roof Books are published by
Segue Foundation / seguefoundation.com
and distributed by
Independent Publishers Group / IPGbook.com